BOSAVI

RAINFOREST MUSIC *from* PAPUA NEW GUINEA

Recorded and annotated by Steven Feld

A collaborative production of Smithsonian Folkways Recordings and the Institute of Papua New Guinea Studies

 Institute of Papua New Guinea Studies

 Smithsonian Folkways Recordings

SFW CD 40487 ℗ © 2001 Smithsonian Folkways Recordings

Weeping

plus poetry

turns

into song.

DISC I: GUITAR BANDS OF THE 1990s

61:56

1	A men's work group clears a new garden	8:40
2	Ulahi sings while scraping sago pith	4:34
3	Ulahi sings while making sago	1:21
4	Fo:fo: and Miseme sing at their sago place	2:17
5	Ulahi and Eyo:bo sing with afternoon cicadas	2:43
6	Ulahi and Eyo:bo sing at a waterfall	6:16
7	Men's vocal quartet with seed-pod rattles	3:31
8	A large men's collective work group sing and whoop	3:16
9	Gaima plays the bamboo jew's harp	1:50
10	Voices in the Forest: a village soundscape	25:06

TABLE OF CONTENTS

ABOVE: *Mt. Bosavi, towering above the forest canopy, as seen from my veranda in 1992. Each view, sound, and aspect of this forest inspires Bosavi song, whose poetic texts are maps of its contours.*

RIGHT: *Separated by a few hours' walk through surrounding forest, each Bosavi village was once dominated by a central communal longhouse and courtyard, like this one at my village in 1990.*

ABOVE: *An early missionary photograph of a Bosavi family, taken in 1964 during the clearing of the Bosavi airstrip. Once established in the area, missionaries encouraged Bosavi people to abandon traditional body adornments like those seen here.*

RIGHT: *Three generations of Bosavi women cast a watchful eye as a pig is ceremonially butchered and distributed, 1976.*

ABOVE: Halawa has his face painted for a gisalo ceremony, 1984.

RIGHT: A group of drummers perform for the Bosavi Dictionary party, 1999.

LEFT: *Gaso, one of Bosavi's best drummers and drum-makers, in the up and down motion that transforms a dancer into a bird at a forest waterfall, 1982.*

RIGHT: *Gigio, whose closeup image is on the cover, was another prominent Bosavi drummer in 1982.*

Song that moves men to tears, 1984. Overcome by grief by a performance, the weeper throws himself onto the dancer.

Weeping moves women to song, 1966. Women traditionally performed their sung-weeping laments seated around the deceased, who was suspended in cane loops over a fire.

Three generations of Bosavi men get their first astonished view of a helicopter in 1984, the dawn of the oil exploration era in Bosavi. In the center is Kiliya:, who had a prominent role in early contact in Bosavi. He is the father of Gaso, one of Bosavi's most notable drummers, and grandfather of Oska, a string band leader.

Bosavi people first heard themselves on cassette when the Institute of Papua New Guinea Studies published Music of the Kaluli in 1982. The young boy at the left, with his hand on his uncle Ho:nowo:'s cassettes, is Oska, who later became the leader of BVDC and Kemuli string bands.

LEFT: *Yubi often took me into the forest to record the birds, whose importance to both the rainforest soundscape and Bosavi poetry can hardly be overstated. In 1982 we spent many days together gathering the sounds for the "Voices in the Forest" radio program.*

ABOVE: *Ulahi and Eyo:bo nurse their infants while listening to playback of their cicada and waterfall duets, 1977.*

In addition to his participation in ceremonial music,
Gigio had one of the first
ukuleles in Bosavi in 1977.

ABOVE: *Gusuwa String Band in 1999. When I asked Mama if she knew about the song man pictured on her T-shirt, she replied, "No, is he your brother?"*

OVERLEAF: *Ulahi, the featured singer and composer of the Voices of the Rainforest CD, listens to a playback of her songs in 1990.*

INTRODUCTION

If you travel all the way into the interior of Papua New Guinea (PNG) from any direction, you'll ultimately come to the country's Southern Highlands Province. Track inward further still, and you'll reach the Great Papuan Plateau and the region's most dramatic physical feature: Mt. Bosavi, the collapsed cone of an extinct volcano. Just north, in the foothills that ramble six thousand feet below Mt. Bosavi's caldera, lies a vast mid-montane rainforest. This land is home to some two thousand people. Bosavi is their collective name for themselves, their place, and their language. Yet because they are spread apart over a varied terrain, Bosavi people also identify deeply with their distinct localities, often using the more specific names Ologo, Kaluli, Walulu, and Wisesi to refer to their regional identities and linguistic dialects.

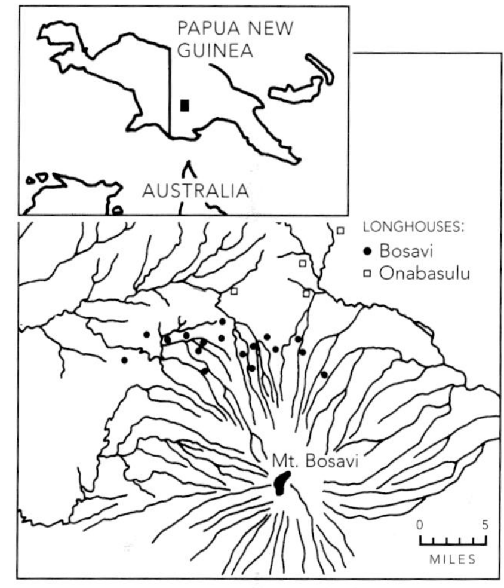

THE GREAT PAPUAN PLATEAU

Across their landscape, Bosavi people have traditionally lived in collective longhouse communities, each separated by an hour or two walk through surrounding rainforest. Everyday social life in Bosavi involves domestic activities in these communities and travel by foot through surrounding forests. There Bosavi people pass the time with family and friends on familiar trails, and work in large gardens that produce varieties of bananas, green vegetables, and local specialties, like pandanus and breadfruit. Also in the surrounding rainforest they fish, hunt, and make sago, their staple starch food, from wild palms that grow in swampy areas around shallow streams.

These longhouse communities, forest trails, gardens, and streams are the settings of the recordings I've collected here. Featured are the voices of the two generations of composers and

"

musicians with whom I've studied during several visits to Bosavi between 1976 and 1999. The musical forms you'll hear represent an extraordinary period in the life of a Papua New Guinean community. They range from music of completely unique local invention, to music born of local contact with geographically contiguous styles, to the first intercultural and hybrid music that connects Bosavi to both the larger Papua New Guinea scene and to the popular string band music of the South Pacific region.

Disc I begins with contemporary guitar bands and the voices of the youngest generation of Bosavi musicians and composers. Disc II features their parents in informal singing and sound-making during daily work and relaxation. This same generation, as well as some of their elders who have since passed on, are featured on Disc III, which presents ritual and ceremonial music. Included there are performance styles ultimately abandoned as a result of the social upheavals experienced in Bosavi during the 1970s and 1980s.

In the notes that follow I use a long-standing spelling convention for Bosavi words. This is the typographic addition of two vowel symbols, a: and o:. The a: symbol represents the initial sound in the word "every," and the o: symbol represents the initial sound in the word "ought." If you take a moment to sound out the vowels with the English guide below, it will be easy to speak and hear the Bosavi words as you read the notes.

FRONT, FROM HIGH TO LOW

i as in beet
e as in bait
a: as in bet
a as in bother

BACK, FROM HIGH TO LOW

u as in boot
o as in boat
o: as in bought

"We're

just

singing

our feelings."

DISC I: GUITAR BANDS OF THE 1990s

How to begin an anthology of twenty-five years of field recordings, of two generations of composers and musicians, of a remote music world that has only recently absorbed the influence of the world beyond its immediate boundaries? The best starting point is the present moment, and to hear it is to celebrate the newest sensation in Bosavi music: the guitar band sound.

This is the music of the first generation of Bosavi people to grow up in an independent Papua New Guinea. It is also the music of the first generation of Bosavi people to grow up with evangelical missionization central to their everyday lives. This is a generation largely stripped of the ritual and ceremonial knowledge and practice of previous generations. It is also the first generation to grow up with access to grade-six education, and with the sporadic presence of anthropologists, development workers, politicians, and agents of the Papua New Guinea state. It is the generation of twenty-five- to thirty-year-olds at the turn of the millennium. Recorded in 1998–99 (tracks 1–10) and 1994–95 (tracks 11–19), the songs on this disc trace the very first waves of stylistic development in the Bosavi string band scene.

This music originates in Bosavi's recent contact history. Western song forms and vocal harmonies were first introduced through hymns taught by the expatriate evangelical missionaries who arrived in 1970. Guitars and ukuleles began trickling into the Bosavi area soon after, at about the time of Papua New Guinea's independence in 1975. The instruments came with Bosavi men returning from early labor contracts in the highlands or coast, or with the first Papua New Guineans from outside Bosavi coming to work at the airstrip's new mission clinic.

This was also the time when the first portable radio-cassette players appeared in the area, also with returning laborers. With these came the first cassettes of the popular music then circulating in PNG's towns. Among the few national groups to get a hearing, Bosavi people particularly liked the PNG string band sounds of Paramana Strangers and New Krymus. The few available cassettes were played until they disintegrated. There was no local source of new cassettes, and only very occasionally did new ones appear with returning workers. Likewise, the combination of a weak signal and poor reception over the mountains from Radio Southern Highlands, sixty miles northeast to Mendi, and few batteries to power the few cassette players meant that Bosavi people heard relatively little of the developing idioms of post-independence PNG popular song circulating in the highlands or coastal communities.

Despite local interest in the new musical possibilities brought by guitars and Western song forms, string band activities were slow to get started in Bosavi. The key factor was the hostility to secular music by the expatriate missionaries and local pastors. For them song was simply a vehicle for evangelical texts, and guitars were only tolerated as accompaniment of mass voices in church. For this reason a secular string band movement didn't gain momentum in Bosavi until the opening, in 1985, of the new community school and airstrip built by the national government. This took place at Muluma, in the central or Kaluli area, three hours' distance from the Bosavi mission station.

String band performance became a mainstay of school events at Muluma. Like the local sports teams that also emerged there at the same time, each group was identified by its longhouse community of origin. The bands typically consisted of four or five voices, with lead, rhythm, and bass guitars, and ukulele. Some used two-part vocal harmony and octave doubling, and the lead voice often sang in a falsetto. The vocal sound was typically strident, following the missionary model of singing as loudly as possible in church. It took some time for the groups to blend their voices to the softer sound of the guitars.

Beginning in 1986 string bands competed for small cash prizes at Independence Day celebrations held at Muluma. While an inter-village competitive spirit was promoted by these events, the members of these bands taught one another what they knew and shared the few available instruments. Students who went out to provincial high schools in the late 1980s brought back new skills and instruments, accelerating the learning of those at the local schools.

The bands that formed at Muluma school and competed there in the late 1980s and into early 1990s are the basis of the current Bosavi string band scene. Now, however, some of the men who started these groups are married, and a husband-wife team leads three of the prominent groups in the region. In each case the woman takes the lead vocal role, and her husband the role as lead instrumentalist and harmony vocalist. Most of the songs are also composed by the men; at this point only one Bosavi woman is active as a guitar band composer.

Experiences of the PNG world outside Bosavi, including provincial high school and town work, are emerging topics; boy-girl relationship and sweetheart songs are popular in the new texts. Lyrics in both Bosavi and Tok Pisin (Melanesian pidgin), with occasional bits of English, are also now common. Some of the groups are experienced as well at singing church hymns, and some songs are modeled on them, either providing new texts to the hymn melodies or secularizing existing texts. But what is most remarkable is how the string band songs continue to develop many of the poetic conventions and topics long central to ceremonial and everyday vocal song in Bosavi. Themes of hunger, of hospitality, of sharing, of loss, and of remembrance are expressed through locally familiar metaphors. Unquestionably, the guitar band movement continues and embellishes the Bosavi tradition of valuing song for its emotional power and poetic appeal.

This sense of historical continuity is even referenced by the name for this new music. Very few Bosavi people ever call it "string band," the general PNG name. Instead they localize the style with the name *gita gisalo*. *Gita* is the Bosavi pronunciation of "guitar." *Gisalo* means "song" and "ceremony" in the Bosavi language; it is also the name of the most important original poetic song and ceremonial form once performed in the region (heard on Disc III, tracks 4 and 5).

Most of the string band groups heard here use two, sometimes three vocal parts. Instrumentally, all groups feature a lead guitar and at least one rhythm guitar, called the "strike." The lead plays introductory and interlude monophonic lines, and the strike strums chords. A ukulele sometimes plays an alternate rhythmic strum. When there are enough guitars, one will be dedicated to the bass role, typically played on just two strings.

As a bass alternative, the "kero" drum has been an occasional part of the string band sound since the late 1980s. It is made from an empty two-gallon metal petrol or kerosene drum, typically brought into Bosavi by men who worked on the regional oil pipeline project. A thick piece of rubber hose is stretched all the way around the drum and across the open spout hole. The player plucks the rubber hose, and the instrument provides a low bass sound, easily tuned to the sixth guitar string, common to all chords. Some groups also use the Bosavi lizard skin head drum (*ilib*) to provide a deep pulse. Others add a tambourine (a church introduction in the 1980s) or the seed-pod rattle (*sologa*), or a contemporary variant of it, a tin fish can partially filled with small pebbles.

In the list of performers that follows you will notice the presence of both English and Bosavi personal names. Missionaries and schoolteachers began to encourage Bosavi pupils to take

English names in the 1970s, and since that time many young people in Bosavi have either been given or have themselves added English or English-derived names. In some cases these approximate the sounds of their Bosavi names, in other cases they are completely unrelated. Additionally, when using Bosavi names, many people now use two, their given name followed by their father's given name. This is another practice increasingly common in the last thirty years, introduced by mission, school, and government record-keeping regimes.

Finally, Bosavi songs never had names or titles. But the guitar band groups, in another innovation, have developed the practice of referring to each distinct song by its opening words. These are presented here in English translation as the song titles for these nineteen guitar band tunes.

DISC 1: NOTES BY TRACK

KEMULI STRING BAND

Rebeka (Sibalame Daibo), lead vocal; Oska (Odo Gaso), lead guitar, vocal harmony; Kenneth (Gaso Wano), strike; Nalex (Nabo Gaso), strike; Thomas Mo:sawo:, bass guitar; Obei Gaso, kero drum bass

Kemuli, led by Oska, is the most acclaimed string band in Bosavi right now and is well known for its innovations in guitar band poetry and performance style. Oska's wife Rebeka plays a prominent role as the lead singer, and is also the first woman to compose guitar band songs in Bosavi.

Heard here are five of the most popular Kemuli songs of the late 1990s, all performed by the group at a 1998–99 New Year's Eve concert. Apart from the dramatic power of Kemuli's poetry, the performance of these songs was quite moving to everyone present for another reason; Rebeka had just given birth to twins, thirty-six hours earlier!

1. My father, my heart

    my father, my heart
    my father, where has he gone?

crying *ya:-* my father is not coming
when afternoon is passing
when the sun is going down
it sounds like my father is calling out
in the afternoon I listen secretly
but there is no talk going on
crying *ya:-* my father is gone for good

Oska composed this song in 1997 after the death of Gaso, his father. It has several times moved listeners to tears and is among the most memorable *gita gisalo* songs composed thus far. Like other new songs, this one continues the tradition of using ceremonial song poetics to evoke memories of the deceased.

The song's most powerful innovation is in the use of sound syllable *ya:-*. This syllable represents the sound of the crying voice; it is the onomatopoeic root of the Bosavi verb for "cry" (*ya:lab*). When Oska and Rebeka sing the syllable *ya:-*, they simultaneously imitate the vocal break of the crying voice. This makes Bosavi listeners think of the sound of the sung-weeping of funerary laments for the recently deceased.

Oska told me that in his father's day Bosavi people could turn crying into song and song into crying. "I'm coming back to that one, the way it was in his time," he said. With this innovation Oska fuses into the guitar band format features of the most important vocal genres in Bosavi: the memorial poetry of *gisalo* songs, and the sung-weeping of the *saya:lab* laments. Both of these ritual genres can be heard on Disc III, tracks 1 through 5.

2. Kemuli

Kemuli is the name Oska now uses both for his band and for his family line, and the second song here is one of several he has composed about their sense of alienation, particularly being pushed out of the Bona community. This theme was taken up in earlier times as well, reflected in the poetry of the song Oska sang five years earlier, with BVDC III, on track 15.

Kemuli
our uncles are chasing us out
why are they chasing us out of here?
Kemuli

An innovative feature of the song is the vocal ending, without instruments, something Oska says he first heard on a cassette of a PNG Gulf Province string band. Oska asked that I add the call of the Black Jungle Coucal (*ilai, Centropus menbeki*) at both the beginning and end of the song. This bird calls from deep in the forest well before dawn (heard on Disc II, track 10). Fading its voice into and out of his own, Oska creates another metaphoric reference to the band's sense of distance from the community where they sang.

3. Oh no!

oh no! oh no!
my husband is tricking me
I wanted to go back home
oh no! but I already had come
tricking me, tricking me
my husband is tricking me

Rebeka composed this song about a sad experience, a fight she had with her husband Oska the previous year. She told me the story this way: "We were fighting with words, but then he hit me on the forehead with his fist and I felt blood come to my face. So I was crying and thinking, why did I marry this person, I thought he'd never do something like this. And from there this song came to me. I wanted it to sound like crying, like when you can't believe something is happening to you."

Domestic fighting is a fact of life in Papua New Guinea, and Rebeka's song is the very first in Bosavi to openly express a woman's pain about it. Her anger and shock are made all the more remarkable because she is performing the song together with Oska, who stands accused by its text. When I asked him about participating in Rebeka's public complaint about his behavior, Oska replied, "It's OK, we are just singing our feelings."

4. What we said

> what we said when we were alone together
> what we planned when we were alone together
> just think about it
> when your husband hits you

The issue of domestic fighting also comes up in the text of a song by Oska, performed immediately following Rebeka's complaint. In the early 1990s, before he married Rebeka, Oska was close to another woman, and they talked about marriage. But her parents refused. Oska became really angry, especially after the woman quickly got together with another man, someone Oska didn't particularly like. "So I told her OK, when you are married to someone else, if that person fights with you, then you can think back to what we said to each other."

In the Western popular music genres that take up such themes, songs are imagined to potentially do a variety of things: provide distance from shock, assuage or revive painful memories, or reconcile grieving or angered persons. Here Oska emphasizes the "just think about it" theme of remembrance, adding a dramatic vocal cry break and instrumental stop as the group sings the Bosavi word *asula:bi*, a future imperative. He added: "When my guitar stops, that person will have to think about how she feels; that's when she will remember what we said and planned in the past."

5. My mother

> my mother, how you always walked
> my mother, how you always talked
> after evening falls, after I've thought about it,
> I can only cry
> my mother, where have you gone?
> my mother, why did you die?
> oh no! my mother is dead

Rebeka composed this song about the shock of her mother's death. "Late in the afternoon, when I get hungry, that's when I think about all kinds of things about my mother." Rebeka added that she took some lines from the women's funerary lament, the *saya:lab* (Disc III, tracks 1–3), sung when her mother died, then put them into this *gita gisalo*, one of several she has composed about the loss of her mother (another is performed by her brother's band on track 18).

Gasali Mates II string band

Rose (Ko:lu Gaso), lead vocal; Matias (Weyabu Daibo), bass guitar; Mike (Mewo: Ene), lead guitar; Michael (Hale Bobane), strike; Amos (Yabe Ba:le), tambourine; Yabeolo Sili, backing vocals; Bennet (Biya:ba: Waibo), backing vocals; Yona (Isa:u Kasoba), backing vocals; Tom (Ta:lowa Gulabia), backing vocals; Paul Dauwa:le, backing vocals

Gasali Mates is the Olabia village string band featuring Matias (brother of Rebeka of Kemuli) and Rose (sister of Oska of Kemuli). The lead vocalist/composer pairs of the Kemuli and Gasali Mates bands were thus formed through sister exchange, the marriage system practiced in Bosavi. Oska exchanged his sister Rose to Matias for his sister Rebeka. The two resulting groups are acknowledged as the major forces in the development of guitar band music in the central Bosavi, or Kaluli, region.

Gasali Mates models their style on the sound of some Gulf Province bands they heard on cassette. They are the first Bosavi guitar band to use a church tambourine for percussion accompaniment and to feature a large chorus of backing singers.

6. Really hungry!

> really hungry!
> OBK children are really hungry!
> start fires!
> start fires in order to cook bamboo
> night is falling, cicadas are making their dusk "bulu" sound
> OBK children, let's get going
> let's go
> to our own Gasali bamboo place

OBK stands for Olabia *buskanaka*, the Tok Pisin pronunciation of "bush kanaka," a colonial-era phrase meaning "uncivilized native." This was a term of derision in earlier times, generally associated with condescension toward local villagers by both their colonial masters and more educated New Guineans.

BK is now a widespread joking and self-deprecating acronym among the young men of Bosavi. The names KBK, OBK, BBK, DBK, and GBK are sung in various guitar songs, referencing the different groups and their villages of origin. The regular use of BK in these song texts typically refers to the sense of marginality felt by young people, particularly men, in Bosavi today. Away from home, in the towns of PNG, they consider themselves to be unsophisticated and uncomfortable intruders in a risky world. And once back in their own villages they have no chance to use any of the new knowledge or skill they have acquired either at school or work.

This is an early Gasali Mates song, using themes of hunger and food, and the metaphoric equivalence of churning stomachs and dusk cicadas. Like many Bosavi songs composed at Muluma community school, this one relates a local village identity to a distinctive food. *Kabulo:* is an edible bamboo delicacy that is plentiful in the Olabia community but not so available in several of the surrounding areas.

Lus Mangi Grin Neks string band

Lus Mangi is the first string band to form at Sibalema village, about three hours west from the Muluma airstrip and school. In Tok Pisin the name Lus Mangi means "lost boys," and Grin Neks ("green necks") is a reference to green-label short-necked bottles of South Pacific brand beer. This is a very exotic item, not only unavailable in Bosavi but also rarely tasted by anyone in the region. The name is meant as a reference to the marginal, renegade, outsider identity many of the young men of the string band scene try out upon return to Bosavi from periods away at school or work, where they've come into contact with PNG town customs.

7. Sadness

there's sadness, sadness for 1998
why is it sad like that?
we were together in 1998, and it is going out now

Despite the image created by their name, Lus Mangi Grin Neks' best-liked song was full of a very local Bosavi-style nostalgia. Composed and performed on New Year's Eve of 1999, this song reminded everyone gathered of what was passing by in their midst — the end of the year 1998. Taking a prominent theme in the history of Bosavi song, of the immediacy of loss and the sadness of memory, the song shows how even in the simplest form, the theme of feelings for the recent past can animate group sentiment. This song noticeably moved the audience. In the following weeks everyone repeatedly asked for its playback and requested that I put it on a compilation cassette of the best new songs for local circulation.

DIFALASULU STRING BAND

Daniel (Daibo Tulunei), lead vocal and strike; Hale Tulunei, lead guitar and backing vocal; James (Diwa), strike; Max (Ayaga: Ba:seyo), kero drum bass; Da:ina Ayaga:, backing vocal

Difalasulu is the current version of the band formerly known as BBK, heard later on tracks 16 and 17. Its leaders are brothers Daniel and Hale, sons of Tulunei and Eyo:bo (heard on Disc II, tracks 5 and 6).

8. BBK brother

BBK brother, BBK brother
who is out to kill you?
oh, sorry, Kamusi boy

Sung in Tok Pisin, this song is of special significance to the Tulunei family, and is deeply moving to the whole Bona community. Daniel composed it in sadness for the loss of his Bona BK brother Abi, the son of his father Tulunei and of Ulahi (heard on Disc II, tracks 2, 3, 5, 6, and

10, and Disc III, tracks 15 and 16). Abi died in a July 1996 plane crash which claimed sixteen Bosavi lives, the worst local disaster in memory. He was on his way back to work at Kamusi, a clear-cut logging operation south of Mt. Bosavi.

TASI KABULO: STRING BAND

9. E-yo, E-yo

> E-yo, E-yo, I'm ending our friendship
> it's OK, it's all right; your mother refuses to let it go on
> it's OK, it's all right; go find yourself another man

This song, by the first band from Tabili village, also west of Muluma, addresses one of the common themes in the new *gita gisalo*, the development of boy-girl friendships and the pain of parental intervention. Like most of these friendship songs, this one is composed and sung from the male point of view. The opening line directly addresses a girl whose name begins with the sound E. The Bosavi phrase *o:lika:*, "it's really all right," at the beginning of the second and third phrases sounds like the English word "OK" and signifies sad acknowledgment of loss.

GUSUWA STRING BAND

Mama, lead vocal; Nelson (Wano Ba:seyo), lead guitar, harmony vocal; Ho:nowo: Wano, strike; Max (Ayaga: Ba:seyo), backing vocal; Gigiyo Sele, kero drum bass

The Gusuwa (which means "cassowary") band performed for the very first time at the 1998–99 New Year's Eve party. Nelson began playing in the earlier BVDC bands under the tutelage of Oska; he is heard with BVDC II on tracks 12, 13, 14. Recently he married Mama, who comes from Walagu, an Onabasulu village to the north of the Bosavi region. He decided to start this band with her and to take advantage of her ability to sing in Onabasulu, Bosavi, Tok Pisin, and English.

10. Long ago

> long ago, in the past
> Bosavi had no dictionary
> however
> having just made it Steve and Bambi have brought it here
> for that reason
> all of us are happy with Steve and Bambi

Nelson and Mama composed this song together for the party to receive the first dictionary of the Bosavi language, written by Bambi B. Schieffelin and me with five Bosavi collaborators. They sang the words first in the Bosavi language and then in Tok Pisin in honor of the two languages appearing together in the dictionary.

BVDC STRING BAND

Rebeka (Sibalame Daibo), lead vocal; Oska (Odo Gaso), lead guitar, vocal harmony; Kenneth (Gaso Wano), strike; Salen (Seligiwo: Degelo:), bass guitar; Nabo Gaso, ukulele; Go:bo: Gaso, backing vocal

BVDC stands for Bona Village Development Committee, a local organization charged with development initiatives. But the acronym came to have a larger life for Bona clan members living at Bolekini in the mid-1990s, signifying how young people there were asserting new agendas, ideas, and desires in the community. Oska named his band BVDC as a way of aligning guitar band activities with the social transformations taking place in the central Bosavi area at the time.

11. Father, mother

> father, mother, convert
> right now, not tomorrow
> brother, sister, convert
> here and now, not tomorrow
> not just for us

all places in PNG
have already converted

Rebeka and Oska met at Muluma school but developed their sound by singing together in the church at Olabia village, Rebeka's home community. There they heard this song, composed by a pastor in Tok Pisin, the Papua New Guinea lingua franca. Oska translated the text into the Bosavi language and developed the melody. The group sings the song first in Tok Pisin and then in Bosavi. The text, about the urgency of conversion, repeats one of the most common themes in the history of Bosavi evangelical sermons.

BVDC II STRING BAND

Rebeka (Sibalame Daibo), lead vocal; Oska (Odo Gaso), lead guitar, vocal harmony; Kenneth (Gaso Wano), strike; Salen (Seligiwo: Degelo:), bass guitar; Nelson (Wano Ba:seyo:), ukulele

12. Where has my mother gone?

Oska leads one of his earliest songs, about feeling fear and hunger when he couldn't find his mother at home and didn't realize she had gone to her gardens. The text repeats, "Where has my mother gone?" and calls out to her, "I'm really hungry."

13. Rosi, Rosi

Rosi Rosi
why are you still sleeping?
you just keep sleeping like you don't hear me asking
I'm hungry, day is coming, get up

Rosi is Oska's nickname for his wife Rebeka. When she and Oska were still getting to know one another, her brother Matias told Oska to come and stay at the family house. When Oska woke the next morning, Rebeka was still sleeping. He called to her, expecting her to rise and cook some food. When she didn't, he composed this song in surprise.

14. Blue mountain

blue mountain
I'm feeling sorry
Mt. Bosavi is my place
why did I leave my home and go away?

Oska's cousin Kenneth (Gaso Wano) plays lead on this Tok Pisin song he composed in 1993 after he left Bosavi to attend Koroba High School. Feeling alone and scared in his new surroundings, he sang about missing his place, and wondered why he left it. On clear days Mt. Bosavi has a blue cast to it, and the opening phrase is a nostalgic and sentimental one for Bosavi people far away from home, as it is for many of the PNG highlanders Kenneth met at high school.

BVDC III STRING BAND

Rebeka (Sibalame Daibo), lead vocal; Oska (Odo Gaso), ukulele, vocal harmony; Kenneth (Gaso Wano), strike; Salen (Seligiwo: Degelo:), lead guitar; Osolowa Gaso, lizard-skin drum (ilib)

15. Sorry, my sister! You people go!

This track, by a third variant of the BVDC group, consists of two songs, the first composed by Rebeka and the second by Oska, edited together at their suggestion. Both were composed at the same moment, recorded in sequence, and address the same theme.

Oska's father, Gaso, was involved in an adultery accusation, and as a result some members of the Bona community angrily demanded that Oska and Rebeka's entire family leave the village to live elsewhere. Rebeka's song addresses the woman alleged to be involved with her father-in-law, expressing astonishment that she wouldn't realize how her actions could be so hurtful to others. Oska's song asks "where will we go?" because his family left their homelands in his grandfather's time, and moved to Bona's lands. Having grown up there, he identifies with no other place. Both songs brought tears to the eyes of Bona people, who, despite their considerable anger at Gaso, also felt real sorrow for Oska and Rebeka's predicament.

BBK STRING BAND

Ho:we Bamo, lead vocal; Daniel (Daibo Tulunei), strike; Nelson (Wano Ba:seyo), lead guitar; Salen (Seligiwo: Degelo:), bass guitar; Hale Tulunei, ukulele; Bage Tulunei, lizard-skin drum (ilib); Yogodo Tulunei, backing vocal

16. Air Niugini plane

17. One time

BBK is the early version of the current Difalasulu group. The group is led by brothers Daniel and Hale, whose sister Mobia is married to a man from Fogomayu, a Kasua community more than a day's walk to the southeast. When Ho:we Bamo, a new relative from Fogomayu, visited Daniel and Hale's family, BBK requested a recording with him as their leader to mark the occasion. None of the BBK members could tell me the meaning of the first song in the Kasua-language, only, following its first words, that it was about an Air Niugini airplane. This strongly marks the song's local exoticism. Air Niugini, the PNG national carrier, flies planes to the towns of Tari, Moro, and Mendi, all twenty-five to sixty miles from Bosavi. But few Bosavi people have been to one of these places, and far fewer have been on an Air Niugini airplane. The second song is sung in Tok Pisin, but its theme and meaning are only locally relevant to Ho:we Bamo, the leader.

GASALI MATES STRING BAND

Rose (Ko:lu Gaso), lead vocal; Matias (Weyabu Daibo), lead guitar; Isamo, bass guitar; Michael (Hale Bobane), strike; Albert, ukulele; Amos (Yabe Ba:le), backing vocal; Joseph, backing vocal

This song was composed by Rebeka (of the BVDC and Kemuli groups) and taught to her brother Matias, the leader of Gasali Mates. The song remembers the death of Rebeka and Matias' mother, and was performed often in the mid-1990s by both BVDC and Gasali Mates.

18. The sun is setting

the sun is setting
at the western side
the sun is setting
why did my mother die?
I didn't eat morning food yet
the sun is setting

Rebeka told me that this song came to her one afternoon as she sat on her verandah watching the sun go down. As she watched, she was thinking to herself that, if her mother were alive, she would have had food first before going off to fill water tubes. No translation could possibly convey the local power of Rebeka's use of metaphors and memorial poetry here. In the new guitar band format, she has created a song with the power typical of Bosavi women's funerary laments (heard on Disc III, tracks 1–3).

19. My sweetheart

my sweetheart
when will you come to my house?
someday I'll be waiting at my house
so just come there

Matias composed this song when he was in high school. The text is typical of the boyfriend-girlfriend songs of the 90s that sing about the desires of young people to get together, talk alone, and get to know one another outside of parental and family pressures. The word *himu* means "heart" in Bosavi, but in the context of these friendship songs is a term of address meaning "sweetheart" and has the same tenderness of the phrase "my baby" as heard in Western popular songs.

l i f t

u p

o v e r

s o u n d i n g

DISC II: SOUNDS AND SONGS OF EVERYDAY LIFE

When you live in a Bosavi village, it doesn't take long to realize that soundmaking is a key feature of everyday work and recreation throughout the community. Acts of assertion, affection, and appeal are constant features of the daily social interactions I've experienced in Bosavi, and their public display is often demonstrably vocal and instrumental. Sentiments and nostalgias, energies and emotions are constantly projected into public auditory space.

The kinds of everyday sounds I'm speaking about are largely spontaneous. You typically hear them when walking trails with friends, when visiting gardens and sago places, or when stopping by familiar village locales where people are working, cooking, or just passing the time with family. These are the sounds of people living and working together. And they are the sounds of people interacting with the surrounding rainforest environment and the pulse of its ever-present insects, birds, frogs, rains, winds, and watercourses.

The second disc of this anthology begins with this very social and public life of the Bosavi sound world. Included are the sounds of communal work by men clearing a garden and making a bridge (tracks 1, 8); of women making sago (tracks 2, 3, 4); of playful song and relaxation recorded in gardens and villages (tracks 5, 6, 7, 9). These recordings were made in 1977, and I continued to hear and record performances and sounds like them in the 1980s and 1990s. Unlike Bosavi's ritual and ceremonial music, which declined seriously from the 1970s due to evangelical missionization, the world of everyday music heard in work, leisure, and other informal contexts has generally remained vibrant. To provide an even stronger sense of how informal sounds and songs of work and leisure shape the feel of everyday life, track 10 is a composite soundscape, a twenty-four-hour day in the life of a Bosavi village, recorded in 1982.

DISC II: NOTES BY TRACK

1. A men's work group clears a new garden

A group of fifteen men cut and fell trees to clear a forest ridge for banana gardens. As they work, a flurry of whoops, yodels, yells, and cheers blends with the sounds of birds, axes, machetes, falling trees, and work commands. Shouts and jokes lead one group into mildly competitive cutting of a tree, while nearby men take a breather, rhythmically shouting "Watch it…watch it!"

Occasionally the exuberance of group work leads directly into bursts of song. As soon as one voice begins, several others join in a split second later, overlapping in the style Bosavi people call "lift-up-over sounding" (*dulugu ganalan*). The layered vocal textures blend with the echoing axe hits, the surrounding birds, and the pulsing of cicadas.

2. and 3. Ulahi sings while scraping pith from a sago palm

The popular song style called *heyalo* originated as a men's ceremonial performance. But the song form has always had quite a public life outside of that original ritual arena. Even though no ceremony had been performed for six years, I recorded more than one hundred *heyalo* songs in 1976 and 1977, all sung in informal work settings. Women participated extensively as composers of *heyalo* and sang them often when they worked in their gardens or at their sago places.

At the time of these recordings Ulahi had composed about ten *heyalo* and had a repertoire of twenty that she often sang when she worked. Here she is scraping sago pith with a heavy stone pounder from a newly felled and split palm. She is sometimes assisted in the scraping by her daughter Yogodo, who is sitting next to her and holding Bage, Ulahi's new baby. Ulahi's song begins with a burst of energy and enthusiasm. As the stone scraper gets heavier and the demanding work more tiring, her pace slows and her voice becomes breathier.

Heyalo songs are shaped like a tree. They have two sections, a "trunk" (*mo:*), which is a refrain, a repeating melody and text. This alternates with "branches" (*dun*); these are verses, a second melody, each time with a slightly modified text. Like a tree, a *heyalo* song "branches" out from its "trunk" by alternations of the verses and refrain.

In Ulahi's first song, one of her favorites, the refrain is "oh, my grandmother" (*wo: ni nuwo*).

It is followed by two sets of paired verses, the first of which questions "Grandmother, where are you going to sleep?" The second answers, "I'm going to ___ " and "I'm hungry at ___," each time inserting new names of land, water, or sago places. By changing these place names with each line, the song's successive branches create a "path" (*tok*). This song path is a poetic map of locations whose naming recalls memorable personal experiences.

Bosavi composers typically made their audiences sentimental by constructing these song paths to evoke memories of places left behind, and of the deceased friends and relatives associated with those places. Since the spirits of the dead, the "gone reflections" (*ane mama*), typically reappear in the treetops as birds, songs follow forest paths from a bird's flight perspective, rather than from the perspective of a person walking local trails.

The second song was composed by Ulahi in the late 1960s when her husband Tulunei was away from Bosavi on a labor contract. The refrain, "my waterway cicada" (*nimo seyalen*), evokes the sound of hungry cicadas heard from a stream. The verses that branch out from the trunk then name the places, trees, and creeks from which the cicadas call out to their brother. The afternoon sound of buzzing cicadas is a conventional metaphor for families gathering to socialize and eat after work. Ulahi's song uses images of hunger and place to evoke her husband's distance from home and her own sense of loneliness and loss.

4. Fo:fo: and Miseme sing at their sago place

Relaxing together while taking a break from scraping sago pith one afternoon, Fo:fo: and Miseme sing a *heyalo* song about the call of the Golden Whistler (*doloso:k, Pachycephala pectoralis*). The song's trunk names the bird and its characteristic whistle sound (*yu*). The alternating sets of branches locate the bird's whistling in local places and trees. Once again, the progression of named places creates a textual path of familiar lands, evocative of deeply held feelings and memories.

Miseme's new husband Da:ina is scraping sago pith nearby. As he hears the song, he begins to scrape in metric accompaniment, and then adds whistled imitations of the *doloso:k* bird's sound. The overlapping, alternating, and interlocking texture of the two voices, the whistling, and the stone scraper rhythm creates a rich "lift-up-over sounding."

5. Ulahi and Eyo:bo sing with afternoon cicadas

In the 1970s the song style called *ko:luba* was neither as popular nor as widely known as *heyalo* in the central or Kaluli area of Bosavi where I lived and made the majority of my recordings. But some women with family ties to the Ologo or eastern Bosavi area, where *ko:luba* was a more historically significant genre, also liked to sing them. Ulahi was born in this area, and composed and sang *ko:luba* as often as she sang *heyalo*.

In the first song, Ulahi greets the arrival of the afternoon cicadas (*alen*) with an improvised *ko:luba* song. She uses poetic sound words like *da: da:*, *siya siya*, and *wa wo:* both to imitate and sing in sonorous counterpoint to the swells of surrounding cicada sound. In a second song, Ulahi and her co-wife Eyo:bo sing about Mt. Bosavi. The sonic interplay of the vocal sounds and cicada sounds in these two songs illustrates how Bosavi women both sing with the forest and respond to it as a source of poetic and musical inspiration.

6. Ulahi and Eyo:bo sing at a waterfall

At a new garden area above a waterfall and pool, Ulahi and Eyo:bo sing together while taking a break to breastfeed their infants. Some of their older children continue to clear the surrounding brush. Singing into the rock pool, their voices playfully overlap and echo in a "lift-up-over-sounding."

The first song was performed earlier by Ulahi as a solo (track 2, "oh, my grandmother," *wo: ni nuwo*).

In the second song the trunk goes: "As my water flows, I will see the gushing white currents." Each of the following branches notes the places, trees, birds, and waterways that call out beyond the flowing water. This song was composed in the late 1960s when a small group of Bosavi men left the area on a labor contract. By constructing the song's path with names of birds, waterways, and places that are very far away, on the borders of or beyond Bosavi, the composer evocatively moved the audience to feelings of sadness for those who had gone.

In the third and final song the trunk image is of a small Ornate Fruitdove (*iya:u, Ptilinopus ornatus*) that hovers at a creek. The branches name a sequence of longhouse sites and the main tree landmarking each, from which the bird calls "I won't be coming back." Each of these repetitions also begins with a different kin term. The composer likened the children of Bosavi to fruitdoves flying away to the new school opened in the early 1970s by missionaries at the first Bosavi airstrip. The birds stop at each village on the way, calling back to their mothers, fathers, sisters, and brothers to say "I won't be coming back." The theme of loss was pushed to its emotional limit by this song, and it remains one of the most memorable texts in all of Bosavi.

These last two songs were particularly meaningful to Ulahi and Eyo:bo. Their husband Tulunei was away with the contract labor group when the first one was initially performed. Additionally, their family resisted missionization in the 1970s, and both Ulahi and Eyo:bo refused to send their children to the mission school at the airstrip, some three hours away from their village.

7. Men's vocal quartet, with seed pod rattle accompaniment

Kulu composed this song and taught it to his friends Gigio, Seyaka, and Kogowe as we all sat around the tape recorder one afternoon. At that time Kulu was temporarily living with me in Sululeb village. With no close relatives there, he said that singing and listening to songs with us made him nostalgic for his home. The trunk of his song yearns, "Mother, I'm alone with no family," and the alternating branches cite place names from the immediate area surrounding my house. Kulu sings the lift-up-over lead in the plaintive bird voice register that reminds Bosavi listeners of the voice of fruitdoves (particularly *muni* and *kalo*, *Ptilinopus pulchellus* and *Ptilinopus perlatus*). The accompanying voices are in a lower vocal register, and all four singers shake seed-pod rattles (*sologa*) as they sing, creating a densely textured pulse that mixes closely with their voices.

8. A large men's collective work group sing and whoop

I made this recording from a high ridge above a forested area. Below me, some eighty-five men from five longhouse communities were dragging enormous logs from the forest to a river gorge to build a bridge. Often, before a difficult pull over a rough stretch of land, a voice would spontaneously break into song. The rest of the group would instantly echo the sound far through the forest. At the end of each song the group intones a dramatic whoop called *ulab*, a term that means "saying *uu*." This kind of orchestrated whooping always ends with a lengthy drone where the voices come together on *oooo*; then they break the drone by stomping in place and shouting a final *uu!* Galvanizing the strength to participate in physically demanding work, the sound of *ulab* marks the dramatic presence of collective male energy. Bosavi people associate this display with another prominent sound symbol of male vitality, the booming *bu kuu!* voice of the Harpy Eagle (*usulage, Harpyopsis novaguineae*).

The first *heyalo* song was composed in 1967 by a man who left his home to live in another village. The trunk image is the departing call of the Black Jungle Coucal (*ikelo:* or *ilai, Centropus menbeki*). The branches name the places he is leaving behind. The second song was composed in the early 1970s by a young man upon return to Bosavi from a two-year labor contract on the coast. The song text names Balimo, Port Moresby, Mt. Hagen, and Rabaul, all major cities he has seen but left behind to return home. At the end of the whooping someone yells "*em tasol, pinis,*" a Tok Pisin phrase meaning "that's all, it's finished." In 1977 use of Tok Pisin was quite restricted in Bosavi; its use here symbolizes the particular circumstances of young men who had labored out side the area and learned to speak the lingua franca of Papua New Guinea's towns.

9. Gaima plays the bamboo jew's harp

Bosavi men say that Huli people who live to their north introduced the bamboo jew's harp (*uluna*) to them long ago. Prior to this introduction Bosavi men played a single-stringed mouth bow as a solo vehicle. Unlike other regions of Papua New Guinea, no elaborate tradition of playing the jew's harp ever developed in Bosavi, and no extensive musical or social symbolism was ever associated with it.

The jew's harp is the only solo instrument played in Bosavi. Youngsters also entertain themselves creating a similar sound with a live sago beetle (*ha:mu*). Attached to a small piece of pliable bamboo, the beetle is dangled in front of the mouth while the player produces vocal overtones to its buzzing wing beats.

Throughout the 1970s and 1980s the jew's harp seemed to come and go in popularity among young men in Bosavi. Gaima was the only man in my village who always had an *uluna* in his netbag and came by regularly to play and give me lessons. He indicated that his playing was typically inspired by the sound of a particular bird or insect. Most of his pieces usually lasted one to two minutes, with a greater amount of time given over to tuning and adjusting the delicate tension so that the instrument could properly sound without interruption.

A most intimate instrument, only the player hears the sounds and overtones of a bamboo jew's harp at the volume level registered by a recording.

10. Voices in the Forest: a village soundscape

This track, originally a radio program, presents the feel of a twenty-four-hour period in a Bosavi village. Environmental sounds are revealed as both a backdrop to and inspiration for the sounds and songs of everyday life.

We begin well before dawn. Deep in the night, sounds of frogs, bats, crickets, insects, owls, and trilling kingfishers punctuate the winds and mists. An occasional cough is heard from a nearby longhouse, where eighty people sleep.

With sunrise, tree leaves begin to flutter in the wind as birds swell in counterpoint. Pigeons, whistlers, parrots, butcherbirds, grackles, coucals, and birds of paradise announce the dawn. People wake and begin cracking firewood, talking and rustling around to the attendant sounds of domestic pigs and dogs.

By 8 a.m. the village is empty; people have gone off to forest locales. Some men and women are at their sago places making food. Other families are off to weed their gardens and to gather vegetables and firewood. Some men have gone to the bush to fell trees for a communal garden.

Bird, insect, and waterway sounds are everywhere. As people work, they sing along and respond to what they hear around them. Ulahi alternates whistling and singing to a background of bird calls while she and her family make sago; Fo:fo: and Miseme take a break and sing a bird voice at their sago place (heard in full on track 4); men cut trees and whoop to harness energy for the tough work (heard in full on track 8); Ulahi greets the afternoon cicadas with a song full of cicada sound imitations (heard in full on track 5).

By late afternoon people are walking back to the village along forest paths. Their arrival is greeted by a rain storm. Leisurely play in the house follows as food is prepared. As rains and winds subside, there is a flurry of bird sounds before the dusk starts to close in.

Softly and slowly the crickets and early night frogs appear, creating a throbbing sound. By 9 p.m. the texture begins to quiet, with the hissing winds and mists rejoining the crickets and insects of deep night.

This track is a re-edition of *Voices in the Forest*, a soundscape documentary originally produced in 1983 by Scott Sinkler with me for National Public Radio. The program aired on NPR and Pacifica affiliates, then on other North American, European, and Pacific networks, including the Papua New Guinea NBC.

Weeping that

moves women

to song;

song that moves

men to tears.

DISC III: SOUNDS AND SONG OF RITUAL AND CEREMONY

One way to enter the world of Bosavi ritual and ceremonial sound is through a local origin story. In the story a boy and his older sister go together to gather crayfish. The girl catches a few but her brother is unsuccessful, so he begins to beg some from her. She refuses, and he feels dejected. Then he catches a shrimp and puts the shell over his nose, turning it red. His hands become wings, and he begins to cry in the voice of the Beautiful Fruitdove (*muni, Ptilinopus pulchellus*). As he cries out, the sister pleads for him to come and now share her crayfish. But only his cries continue, like the voice of a fruitdove. As he repeats the falsetto melody with four descending tones, the boy-bird adds plaintive words about his sense of loss. Weeping plus poetry turns into song.

At Bosavi funerals women performed wept laments that used the fruitdove melody articulated in this myth. They also improvised texts filled with names of the places where they worked, traveled, and lived together with the deceased. Lament poetry also remembered the acts and situations whose sharing gave everyday meaning to their relationship. While distinctly personal testaments, these laments evoked poignant experiences and social memories common to all Bosavi people.

Examples of group, duet, and solo varieties of funerary weeping (*sa-ya:lab*) open Disc III (tracks 1, 2, and 3). These sounds indicate what was once self-evident in Bosavi, namely, that song poetry originated in the crying voice and in the evocation of bird sound. The role birds assumed as mediators of sound and sentiment was profound here. More than transparent avian presences whose everyday sounds were clocks and tuning forks of the natural world, birds were simultaneously heard as spirits, the "gone reflections" (*ane mama*) of Bosavi dead who had passed on to the treetops. It was as a bird that one reappeared after death, and it was like a bird that one became through the most visceral and stirring sound of the human voice.

While still performed in some Bosavi villages, the practice of funerary weeping has diminished greatly since the mid-1970s. Partly this is a response to government demands for quick burials. Partly, too, it is a response to evangelical Christian intolerance of the ritual; the expatriate missionaries specifically discouraged crying, insisting it was an expression of moral weakness. Additionally, both government and mission impacts promoted male power in Bosavi. With this came greater attempts to control the social criticism women typically voiced in their funerary weeping, particularly their anger about social vulnerability and their veiled accusations about sorcery.

The song born of the mythic weeping that turned a boy into a bird reached its most dramatic form in ceremonies performed by Bosavi men. There were five varieties of these ceremonies, but Bosavi people maintain that they only originated one, named *gisalo*. *Gisalo* is also the generic local term for "song" or "ceremony," equivalent to the term *singsing* in Tok Pisin, the PNG lingua franca.

Of the four lesser ceremonies, one called *heyalo* originated near the Lake Campbell area southwest of Mt. Bosavi; it was quite popular in the 1960s. Another, called *ko:luba*, came from the southeast of Mt. Bosavi and was first performed in the central Bosavi area in 1968. It shared the same costume type as the group ceremonial drumming called *ilib kuwo:*. This kind of drumming preceded an all-night *ko:luba, heyalo*, or *gisalo* ceremony. The two least elaborate ceremonies were *iwo:*, which originated southwest of Mt. Bosavi, and *sabio*, which originated east of the Kikori River. Brought by early government patrol carriers from the Lake Kutubu area, *sabio* was typically performed by youths and young men as a late afternoon prelude to major ceremonies.

The last *gisalo* ceremony in Bosavi took place in 1984 (track 5). *Gisalo* songs were also sung at night for spirit medium seances (track 4); this practice ceased by the end of the 1970s. Brief renditions of *gisalo* are now performed in Bosavi only on September 16th, for the annual Papua New Guinea Independence Day celebration.

The last *heyalo* ceremony in Bosavi took place in 1968; subsequently no ceremonial recording of the style is presented here, only the informal performances of the songs heard on Disc II. The style is still quite popular with a segment of the population over age forty, and is most typically heard as a form of work song in gardens or at sago creeks.

I witnessed and recorded all-night *ko:luba* ceremonies in 1977 (tracks 7 through 10) and in 1982. Since then the ceremony has been staged on just a few occasions, with fragments occasionally performed for Independence Day, typically preceded by a prelude of drumming *ilib kuwo:* (track 6). Everyday varieties of *ko:luba* can also be heard on Disc I; they are still sung for work and leisure by the same older generation that equally enjoys *heyalo*.

Of the lesser ceremonies, men's *iwo:* (tracks 11–14) consisted of a fixed set of about forty-five songs. These were only sung the night before pigs were to be killed. Two varieties of women's *iwo:* songs, called *kelekeliyoba* and *gido:fo agelo:*, were composed anew for each ceremony and sung on the morning of the killings (tracks 15 and 16). This ceremony was last performed in 1969, as was *sabio* (tracks 17 and 18), whose duo or quartet songs were typically sung as a prelude to other ceremonies. As a fixed sequence of songs whose texts were unintelligible to Bosavi people, *sabio* were never locally composed, and thus disappeared as quickly as *iwo:*.

The *gisalo*, *heyalo*, and *ko:luba* ceremonies generally took place from dusk to dawn in a crowded longhouse. The songs were composed and performed by a group of guests for their hosts, meant to make them so sentimental as to be moved to tears. This was largely accomplished by the performance of poetic songs. The texts named forest lands, waters, and trees, and the sounds of special poetic words evoked their sensuous qualities. The result was what Bosavi people called a "path" (*tok*) of metaphoric images, called "turned-over-words" (*bale to*). What Bosavi listeners would hear inside and underneath these turned-over-words provoked them to thoughts about loss and abandonment. This moved them to tears, and, using the same fruitdove melodic contour as laments, provoked wept echoes of the song in progress. Song, in the end, turned into weeping just as forcefully as weeping turned into song.

Such an arresting and confirming response was most typical of *gisalo* and *heyalo* because their poetic paths of named places were intimately familiar to members of the immediate audience. Less moving were *ko:luba* songs, because many of their paths contained unfamiliar and faraway place names from south and east of Mt. Bosavi. Only when composers substituted local places and imagery in these songs did their performances gain a greater affecting power.

DISC III: NOTES BY TRACK

1. Funerary sung-weeping group

October 4, 1976: Within minutes after the discovery of Sa:na:so's death, the people living at Sululeb gathered in their longhouse. Some close friends and relatives were seated around the body, others moved about in shock, and all wept forcefully, the sound filling the house and surrounding area for the following two hours. The least controlled wailing borders on shrieks but occasionally becomes a full falsetto version of the fruitdove cry (the descending melody contour D-C-A-G). Some men were so choked up that they quivered in place, wailing forcefully until others helped them gain some composure. The more plaintive and controlled wailing you hear is the type that is both melodic and texted; this was performed by the women who were closely related to Sa:na:so and who were seated around his body.

The short exhortatory texts register the complete disbelief of the moment: "Wake up, you never slept like this before!" "You're not an old man, don't trick us!" "You were just eating yesterday, are you just asleep?" Other texts, reaching through the shock to reflection, note how Sa:na:so was thin, frail, and had a history of recent sickness. Still others noted now he was going off to the treetops to join his brother Sialo.

2. Funerary sung-weeping by Gania and Famu

At the mourning following the death of Bibiali of Aso:ndo on November 13, 1976, there were several independent but musically interlocked sung-weeping laments (*sa-ya:lab*) by two, three, or four overlapping voices. In the sequence heard here, Gania and Famu each begin with their own personal lament, one weeping to her bridewealth relation (*na:su*) and the other to her father (*aya* or *dowo*). The two women are sitting next to each other, close to Bibiali's body, laid out on the floor at the front end of the longhouse. Other women are also seated around the body, and another one hundred people filled the house, accounting for the ambient level of surround-sound.

Two styles of multi-voiced weeping can be heard. Staggered entrances and completely overlapped voices characterize the first. Following that, one hears a more paced delivery, with the two weepers alternating whole phrases, only overlapping at the beginning and end of their lines. Although improvised, the texts also interlock poetically in a cohesive fashion, with one woman frequently commenting upon or embellishing a remark just made in the other's immediately preceding phrase. One set of themes concerns the lack of solidarity in Bibiali's family. "If you had a son, he would remember you every day" is overlapped by "Your son is a sago palm at Obesana." Lines expressing anger build up throughout the text in this way, focusing on the way death creates a deep sense of vulnerability. In the ensuing dialogues, Gania, Famu, and other women voiced public criticism of ruptured relations in Bibiali's family, as well as spoke to specific experiences and places they shared with him during his life.

3. Funerary sung-weeping by Hane

Hane improvised a long sung-weeping lament to her cross-cousin Bibiali shortly after the previous track. This example typifies the most poetically elaborate and song-like variety of Bosavi weeping. Although Hane is shedding tears and choked up throughout, her melodic and rhythmic consistency, phrase patterns, and poetic cohesion all indicate remarkable control. The textual images chain together, moving over a path of some fifty places Hane and Bibiali had shared in life. Many of these are voiced in poetic formulae of the form "cross-cousin, you and I were together at ____." The text also contains continual reminders that from now on Bibiali will only appear to Hane as a bird in the treetops.

(A transcription and translation of this performance can be found in chapter 3, "Weeping that Moves Women to Song," of my book, *Sound and Sentiment: Birds, Weeping, Poetics, and Song in Kaluli Expression*, University of Pennsylvania Press, 1982/1990).

4. Seance *gisalo* song by Aiba with weeping

While principally composed for and performed at the ceremony of the same name, *gisalo* songs were also sung during spirit medium seances. These were held in total darkness. A medium, lying on his back, was surrounded by an audience who chorused the songs and then verbally interacted with the spirit who sang them. Throughout the seance the medium would leave his body to roam an invisible realm, a reflection of the visible world. Spirits of the dead and of forest places came up through his mouth to converse with the audience. In between these conversations, the spirits about to emerge or depart sang a *gisalo* song through the medium. The song's poetic text, particularly its place-name path, was a series of clues to the spirit's identity.

Outside the frame of performance, mediums always claimed that they neither composed nor performed these songs. They considered themselves only as vocal conduits for the spirits who came up on them. They frequently acted surprised or much bemused to hear playback of the seance songs they had just "sung."

The song heard here was the second of thirteen sung during a spirit seance featuring the medium Aiba. The spirit voice begins solo, coming up faintly, accompanied by the medium's mussel-shell rattle (*sob*). The distant effect of the soft voice is no doubt enhanced by the rain pounding on the thatch roof of the longhouse, enveloping the attention and anticipation of the audience seated in the darkness. The opening lines identify the singer as a bird, an Ornate Fruitdove (*iya:u, Ptilinopus ornatus*) hovering overhead. As the chorus joins, the spirit voice grows stronger and increasingly yearning. The text unfolds as an intricate path map linking places in the vicinity of Kokonesi longhouse.

The sequence of named places moved Neono to tears when he realized the emergent spirit voice to be Dubo, his deceased son. His weeping continues throughout the last part of the song and past its finish, interlocking with the singing voice of the spirit, the voices of the overlapping chorus members, and the pulse of the rattle. Neono's sung-weeping, like the funerary lament heard earlier, inserts brief texts into the bird-voice melody. Often these words are place names of deep significance to him and his dead son, whom he affectionately calls "my land crab" (*ni handa*). Bosavi people replace personal names with reciprocal food names to mark the special relationship that originates in sharing foods, particularly local delicacies. Use of these terms in song and lament is particularly compelling.

Prominent in the sound of this *gisalo* song is the shell rattle (*sob*), an instrument specific to the accompaniment of this song genre. The rattle consists of about thirty mussel shells strung together and suspended from a string. The string coils at the top around a piece of pencil-thin etched bamboo.

In ceremonial *gisalo* performance, the singer-dancer holds this bamboo handle in his down-stretched hand, close to his side. The shells suspend from the handle, reaching down to the floor just next to his ankle. As the dancer bobs up and down with arms held tight to his side, the rattle lightly lifts up and down, continuously brushing the floor and creating a jingle-jangle pulse. This shimmering sound, likened by Bosavi men to soft water rolling over rocks, marks the pulse of the dancer's up and down movements.

When *gisalo* songs were sung at spirit medium seances, the medium also used the mussel-shell rattle. Lying on his back in the darkness, he held the instrument at his side, tapping it on the house floor. The tapping of the rattle both marks the singer's pulse and contributes to the overall sonic drama during the seance. As the song progresses, the rattle sound gets louder, contributing to the hypnotic and mesmerizing quality of the overall performance.

(A transcription and translation of this performance can be found in chapter 5, "Song that Moves Men to Tears," of my book, *Sound and Sentiment: Birds, Weeping, Poetics, and Song in Kaluli Expression*, University of Pennsylvania Press, 1982/1990).

5. Ceremonial *gisalo* performance by Halawa

From a theatrical as well as poetic point of view, *gisalo* was the most elaborate of the ceremonies once staged in Bosavi. From dusk until dawn, members of a guest community would stage the singing and dancing for a host longhouse. Such events solidified relations between the two communities, celebrating marriages, food distributions, and other formal exchanges and alliances.

The aesthetic appeal of *gisalo* was connected to its dramatic qualities, including its staging, costume, song, and dance. In the dark longhouse, torch light accentuated the dancer's costume, highlighting the sway of cassowary and bird of paradise feathers protruding from his painted face and body. In the rear, palm streamers arched up and over from his shoulders to his heels. The up and down motion of his dance, from the balls of the feet with slightly flexed knees, was sonically and visually enunciated both by the lilting costume and by the mussel-shell rattle. The performer was transformed into a bird dancing in place at a forest waterfall.

This image was both aesthetic and primordial. Because birds were seen and heard as spirits of the dead, their motions and sounds once evoked powerful feelings for Bosavi people.

Additionally, the up and down flow of the *gisalo* dancer mythically originated in the gait of a bird that nests in rock gorges by waterfalls, the Giant Cuckoodove (*wo:kwele, Reinwardtoena reinwardtsi*).

The form of the *gisalo* ceremony was elaborate. Once the evening turned dark, four dancers entered the longhouse and positioned themselves two at the rear and two at the front. Behind them, also at each end of the house, sat a chorus of men. Audience members lined the sides of the longhouse's central corridor.

Alternately from each end of the house, a lone dancer would stand and perform a newly composed song. Dancing in place, he would sing the first portion of each song alone. As the song reached the end of its first section, its "trunk," the dancer would move forward at tempo, in a straight line, all the way down the central corridor to the other end of the longhouse. There, facing the chorus, and again dancing in place, he would sing the concluding section of the song, its "branches." Throughout the branches the dancer would be accompanied by the chorus, who echoed his text and melody a split second later in the echoing style called "lift-up-over sounding." At the close of the song the dancer continued his up and down motion, made a small U-turn, then performed the entire song again, first singing and dancing alone in place, then returning back down the house corridor to face the other chorus and complete the song with their accompaniment.

Gisalo songs always brought forth strong memories and emotions. When overcome with sadness, members of the host audience burst into tears and loud mournful wails that musically overlapped and merged with the song. Then, angered by the grief they had been made to feel, one would grab a resin torch from a bystander and rush out onto the dance floor to jam the flame into the dancer's shoulder. This repayment for the pain of the song would often set off a burst of mass whooping from the crowd, accompanied by stamping feet and snapping bow strings. The dancer continued with total composure, seemingly unaffected by the crying and burning. But from that moment he would bear the shoulder scars that reminded all that his performance had moved another to tears.

Gisalo ceremonies put Bosavi men in the spotlight as ceremonial composers and performers, parallel to the way funerary laments focused on women's performance. But Bosavi women also participated in *gisalo* ceremonies, by performing weeping in response to the songs and staging a welcoming dance called *sosamaya* to mark the arrival of the dancers outside of the host longhouse. Additionally, women orchestrated much of the host-guest interaction, by supervising the cooking and extensive distribution of ceremonial foods before, during, and after the ceremony.

The *gisalo* song heard here was performed by Halawa, shortly after 3 a.m. during a ceremony at Wasu longhouse in 1984. This was the last all-night *gisalo* ceremony staged in Bosavi. The song you hear was Halawa's sixth performance of the night, and like the previous ones, it provoked strong crying from the audience. The recording was made from a loft high in the center of the sixty-foot longhouse corridor; as a result there is an enhanced stereo effect, with the song performed either to the right or left side, and the motion of the dancer down the corridor between the trunk and branches sections.

6. Group ceremonial drumming, *ilib kuwo:*

Hand drums, called *kundu* in Tok Pisin and known locally in Bosavi as *ilib*, were played by costumed dancers as a late afternoon and early evening prelude to all-night ceremonies. Usually two to six drummers participated in the performance, called *ilib kuwo:*. Each performer tuned and drummed while dancing in place with an up and down step. Initially positioned at either end of the longhouse, the drummers then traversed the long central corridor while dancing and playing. Whether alone, in groups of two, or criss-crossing with a drummer or two from the other end of the corridor, the resultant throbbing sound was overwhelming, and definitely got the audience in the mood for the approaching ceremony.

Sometimes drumming also moved listeners to tears, and led an audience member to burn either the shoulder of the drummer, the side of his instrument, or both, in retaliation. The potential for weeping derives from the instrument's distinct sound symbolism. The drum is considered the voice of the Papuan Bellbird (*tibodai, Pitohui cristatus*). Its desired sound is a pulsating imitation of the bird's name, *tibo tibo*, with no gaps or pauses. In the reflection world the *tibodai* bird is the spirit of a dead child. When Bosavi listeners hear the bird voice pulsing *tibo tibo* through the drum, they might also hear a child calling *dowo dowo*, "father, father." It is at that time that they are moved to tears of grieved reflection.

For both the *ko:luba* ceremony and for *ilib kuwo:* drumming, dancers wear a costume that features a crayfish-claw rattle (*degegado*) in the rear of their dance belts. The term *degegado* derives from *dege*, the sound of crayfish claws, and *gado*, the word for the cordyline leaves that are regularly used for the back of the dance costume. The rattle consists of a pliable piece of cane arched out from an erect post; dried crayfish claws are attached to the end in a bundle, with as many as fifty pieces strung together. The crayfish claws jangle together to directly mark the pulse of the dancer's up and down motion. The crisp and punctual sound of the rattles overlaps the thick but continuous pulsing of the drums. The interlocking density of costume, rattle, and drum sound creates the desired aesthetic effect, a "lift-up-over sounding."

With the demise of ceremonialism in Bosavi, drumming is now typically limited to short outdoor presentations at the annual Papua New Guinea Independence Day celebration. But in honor of the presentation of the Bosavi dictionary on January 1, 1999, thirteen men in full *ilib kuwo:* regalia drummed in the Bolekini village courtyard for almost twelve continuous hours! They were accompanied for part of the time by two women who escorted them with the cheering and greeting *sosamaya* dance. This recording was made on that afternoon.

7. through 10. Songs and sounds of the *ko:luba* ceremony

Ko:luba songs and the ceremony of that name were introduced into the central Bosavi area in the mid-1960s by a man named A:siya: from the longhouse community of Wahaleb. When I began to study these songs in 1977, A:siya: was the only person in Bosavi actively composing them. His repertoire consisted of about one hundred songs, of which twenty-five were his own compositions. A:siya: taught three kinds of *ko:luba* songs: duo dance songs (*dasidan*), heard on tracks 7, 8, and 9; refrain songs, (*tai*), heard on track 9, and processional songs (*gulufofi hanan*), heard on track 10.

The *ko:luba* ceremony as taught by A:siya: was performed by eight to twelve costumed dancers. In groups of two they alternated singing throughout the night. Each pair would sing the same song five times per round, at different positions in the longhouse's central corridor. They sang first at the rear end of the longhouse, where the whole group was seated. Next they sang in the middle section, then at the front end, then again at the middle, and then back at the rear end.

Singers faced each other as they sang, bobbing up and down in place, and sometimes holding hands. The crayfish-claw rattle was suspended by a curved bamboo shaft from the rear of each dancer's belt, producing a shimmering background accompaniment pulse. In between rounds of the song, a skipping step would take the dancers from one house position to the next. Songs performed in this way were the major component of the ceremony, and as many as ninety might be performed between dusk and dawn.

At select times another type of song would simultaneously take place. Called *tai* and sung by the ensemble of seated performers, these would begin once a pair of dancers had finished their first round of a song and had moved off to the center of the house to sing it a second time. A fixed corpus of six songs, each *tai* is but a one-line phrase with a similar melodic pattern.

To begin and close the ceremony, and to add to the drama about every ten or more songs, a processional called *gulufofi hanan* took place. Two dancers would begin, and after they had sung their song through, the remaining dancers would rise and quickly join them, parading from one end of the house to the other, singing with overlapping voices. The strutting motion of the procession brought the audience to their feet, whooping and cheering along and snapping bow strings. One particular form of exuberant cheer, done by women in a high falsetto, was called "doing uwo:" (*uwo:lab*). It was a cheer of encouragement, but also taunted the dancers by its vocal imitation of the aroused call of the Riflebird (*uwo:lo, Ptiloris magnificus*), for whom it is named.

The first song (track 7) is sung by A:siya: and Go:bo:. Its text, "my wife" (*ni diyo:*), is about going to sago places to make food. The place names are all from faraway Tulom, south of Mt. Bosavi, and the language is unintelligible to almost all Bosavi listeners.

The second song (track 8) is also sung by A:siya: and Go:bo:. Its text goes: "A long time ago I went there."…. "I went to (land name)…. I went to (water name)." Again, the language and the places cited are exotic to Bosavi listeners.

The third song was sung by Amini and Mei; portions of it can also be heard in an informal version as men work to clear a garden on Disc I (track 1). After singing it the first time through, the dancers stomp off to the middle of the house; the remaining seated performers then sing a *tai* simultaneously with the next performance. The *tai* is sung several times, and its text names leaves and sounds of water sprinkling down them at the places indicated by the first word of each line.

The fourth and final song was sung first by Amini and Gaso, and then joined by A:siya:,

Go:bo:, Agale, Ilailo:, Weinabe, Hawi, and Mei, as they all danced around the house in processional style, to the exuberant whoops and cheers of the onlookers. Loud *uwo:* cheering from the women can be heard as the men pass by them. The song text gives a sequence of distant place and water names and for each says, "It's too hot to walk there."

11. through 16. Songs and sounds of the *iwo:* ceremony

Iwo: is the set of forty-five songs sung the night before a large pig kill. The ceremony had not been performed for ten years when I first arrived in Bosavi. After a time, friends suggested that I consult Ganigi, an elder man of the Nageba:da:n longhouse community, about the songs. He was said to be among the few alive who knew the entire corpus and proper sequence in which they should be sung. By that time severely crippled and unable to walk, Ganigi was enthusiastically carried by relatives to Sululeb, where I was living. Over several days he taught the songs to me and a local group of men so that all forty-five songs could be recorded, transcribed, and permanently available. The songs presented here are numbers three, ten, twenty-two, and twenty-five in the overall sequence of the forty-five, chosen to represent the major musical and textual features of the style.

Seated at the far end of the house and surrounded by a small chorus of Fagenabo, Da:ina, Kulu, and Hawi, Ganigi starts each song by singing the main phrase solo. He is then quickly joined by the overlapping voices of his chorus, and together they repeat the two- or three-line textual formulae of the song. The seated chorus members accompany instrumentally by shaking seed-pod rattles (*sologa*), crayfish-claw rattles (*degegado*), and tapping axe handles on the house floor.

After the first lines are stated, another man, Ba·seyo, joins from the other end of the longhouse. Swinging a large club (*nage*), he hits the floor at the house entrance and then comes dancing down the center corridor toward the area where the singer and chorus sit. He bounces up and down with the club and for each song shouts out the name of a different land or waterway. All of these place names are far north or south of Mt. Bosavi. Ganigi told us that each song should go on in this way for a considerable time, until the leader cues closure with a loud *wo:-i!!* In order to instruct the chorus and record the entire corpus in a single day, Ganigi suggested short versions of each song.

The first song (track 11), like the others in the opening sequence, has a text instructing how the *iwo:* ceremony is done. This one tells how the pigs are placed on a butchering rack (*iwo: togo-batililama:*). The name shouted by the *nage* is Dibiya, a waterway.

The second song (track 12) illustrates another textual pattern indicating names of lands and waters where pigs live (*eba go:dolowa*). The shout is Walina, another waterway.

The third song (track 13) illustrates another melody and text type, recounting the crossing of rivers (*oniyaba suwo*). The shout is Ko:lega, a waterway far to the north near Mt. Sisa, the northern edge of the known world for Bosavi people.

The fourth song (track 14) is the twenty-fifth in the sequence, and beyond this point the order of songs is relatively flexible. The text here utilizes tree and leaf names and poetic words indicating the sounds of the pigs stepping on the leaves in the mud (*guge gugeyo:*). The shout is Sowaya, a faraway land near Yamili.

Women's participation in the *iwo:* ceremony involved about an hour of singing at dawn on the morning the pigs were killed. In the eastern and central Bosavi area the song formula women sang was called *kelekeliyoba*. Place names and pig names were newly inserted in the formula by each new song leader. The rest of the women chorused with a staggered lift-up-over repeat, accompanying with the seed-pod rattle and slight swaying motion in place.

The word *kelekeliyoba* represents sounds of pigs in the mud near sago places. The song text asks: "Are you at __?" (with a different sago area each time) and "Are you __?" (with a different pig name each time). These questions alternate with *kele kele*, an imitation of pig sounds, as well as other words indicating the sounds of pigs eating sago shavings. These nostalgic songs were sung at a slow pace. They were highly evocative of the affectionate bonds between women and their pigs and sago places. This song (track 15) was led by Ulahi; the lift-up-over chorusing voices are Ea, Gania, and Gisa.

The variant of *kelekeliyoba* sung in the western areas of Bosavi was called "counting feet" (*gido:fo: agelo:*). In these songs there are no place names, only pig names inserted into the repeating formula. Counting feet songs all begin with a repeated phrase, *ye wo:*, which is a signal that pigs are on the loose. The next line names a pig and says that its feet are running fast. With each successive turn, the pig name changed. The pacing of these songs varies, and the singers indicated that this imitates the way some pigs run faster than others. This song (track 16) was led by Ea with a lift-up-over chorus of Ulahi, Gania, and Gisa.

17. and 18. Duet and quartet of *sabio* songs

Sabio originated some twenty-five miles east of Bosavi. The songs were taught to Bosavi men by carriers who came in the 1950s on patrols that originated from the colonial government post at Lake Kutubu. The men who served as carriers or police for the colonial government were Foi (from around Lake Kutubu) and Fasu from the area east of the Hegigio or Kikori river, in between the Bosavi and Kutubu groups. The Bosavi men memorized the songs, and a duo, quartet, or sextet of young men would sing them in the late afternoon or early evening as a prelude to a major all-night ceremony.

In the 1970s I found that only those with long-standing family ties to the eastern Bosavi areas knew any *sabio* songs. One elder, Kiliya:, whose ties to the area where the songs come from were significant, taught the songs to his sons Wano and Gaso, who brought several of them into the central Bosavi area in the 1960s. Wano and Gaso occasionally sang as a duet (track 17) and taught songs to other clan Bona men, here Gigio and (their much younger brother) Sowelo, with whom they sang as a quartet (track 18).

In both the duet and quartet versions the singers face each other and alternate lines while bobbing up and down in place and softly shaking the seed-pod rattle (*sologa*). Each phrase is marked by a pair of overlapping voices coming together in a long intoned *oooo*, often with a marked crescendo and decrescendo pattern. The songs are demanding from a performance point of view both because of their pace and high vocal register. Neither Wano nor Gaso could identify the texts or their meanings.

A BRIEF HISTORY OF BOSAVI ENCOUNTERS

Given the variety of musical loss and gain represented in this collection, an obvious question arises: what happened in Bosavi that so dramatically changed the musical culture over a twenty-five-year period? One starting point is European contact with the Great Papuan Plateau. This process began in 1935, when Jack Hides and Jim O'Malley made their Strickland-Purari patrol. The following year the Archbold Expedition flew over Bosavi in preparation for the Bamu-Parari patrol of Ivan Champion and C.I.J. Adamson. This later patrol made the first contact with the Bosavi people; the previous one had passed through the lands of the Onabasulu to the north.

More substantial contact between Bosavi people and outsiders followed World War II, but it wasn't until 1958 that Australian colonial government officers stationed at Lake Kutubu, about twenty-five miles to the northeast, attempted the first regional census. In the following few years the colonial patrol officers used their power to end fighting and pacify the area. In the 1960s a government station was opened at Komo, two days' walk to the north. More regular police patrols followed, and among their effects was the consolidation of Bosavi people into about twenty long-house communities. The colonial government insisted on rest houses in each community, as well as maintenance of outhouses, regulation burial of the dead, severe punishment for incidents of inter-village fighting, and appointment of a local headman in each community. All of these impacts were typical of the "civilizing mission" of the colonial administration in the interior of what were then the Australian territories of Papua and New Guinea.

In 1964, missionaries of the Unevangelized Fields Mission (UFM, later known as the Asia Pacific Christian Mission, or APCM) based in the neighboring Lake Kutubu area spent six months in the eastern Bosavi region. This was the first continuous contact with an outside force, and it was a signal event in Bosavi history. One of the missionaries prepared a first description of the Bosavi language, while the other supervised construction of a sixteen-hundred-foot-long bush airstrip at a place called Waiyu. When the missionaries recruited laborers to clear the forest there, a group of Bosavi men was, coincidentally, in the midst of holding a secret initiation nearby. Fearing that their autonomy and particularly their ritual secrets were now substantially threatened, the Bosavi male elders and initiates abandoned the initiation lodge to work on the airstrip. With this the institution of male initiation ended forever in Bosavi.

Despite sporadic and temporary migration of young men for labor schemes following construction of the airstrip, Bosavi remained distant from the colonial state through the rest of the 1960s. This remained true even after the arrival of a resident expatriate missionary family in 1970, and after Papua New Guinea's independence in 1975. The lack of local roads, of capital infrastructure, of government presence, and of development initiatives all kept Bosavi as physically remote and economically marginal to the new nation as it had previously been to the colony.

During that period one still encountered much in the way of local political and economic autonomy, egalitarianism among adult males, and complementary gender roles in Bosavi. Extensive bonds of friendship, obligation, hospitality, and reciprocity were clearly the major factors in the organization of domestic life, local work, ceremonial activities, hunting and gardening, and bridewealth transactions. Certainly there was little of the "big man" pattern of social organization or the varieties of antagonism between women and men then much written about for the Papua New Guinea highlands. In these ways much of social life in Bosavi through the 1960s and into the 1970s could still be reasonably described with sociological terms like "classless" and "small-scale."

But the dramatic changes brought by evangelical missionization rapidly destabilized autonomy in Bosavi, and with it the accuracy of those terms. When the resident Australian missionaries arrived, they immediately expressed hostility to local rituals. Confident that the forest was filled with satanic spirits, they hardly bothered to learn any of the local cosmology. Bosavi people were openly berated about the evil imagined to live in their environment, their hearts, and their minds. The message was unequivocal: either renounce traditional ways and prepare for the second coming of Jesus Christ, or face the impending hell fire. The message intensified when the expatriate missionaries imported Huli evangelical pastors from the highlands to the north to aid in spreading the gospel. In addition to a particularly zealous style of preaching, the Huli pastors easily intimidated their Bosavi neighbors, to whom they felt both culturally and morally superior. In all these ways, evangelical Christianity initiated a local regime of fear, much remembered today for the guilt and confusion it instilled.

Two uncanny accidents led many Bosavi people to believe that the missionaries held a mystically powerful key to the depths of their language and culture. The first of these was the identical initial sound of the Bosavi word for sorcerer, *se*, and the ubiquitous new mission word, Satan. The second was that a traditional Bosavi story about the world ending in fire resonated clearly with the mission story of hell fire and apocalyptic destruction. Coincidences like these led Bosavi people to willingly take mission dogma quite seriously, despite considerable confusion over the meaning of the Bible stories.

In addition to holding Bosavi people as a captive audience for evangelization, the missionaries also wielded considerable specific powers. These included control of air traffic in and out of the region, and control over access to education, work, and virtually all forms of information, development, and social benefit. This domination took place at a distinct moment in Papua New Guinea's history, a time when the newly independent government's main concern was the development of a national political economy. Policing what missionaries were doing in remote parts of the country was a low national priority, despite widespread reports of cultural destruction.

Indeed, it seemed that the new national government was grateful to missionaries in remote areas for maintaining local airstrips and managing clinics and schools. Consequently, the continued lack of government presence in Bosavi meant that evangelical rhetoric and mission policy was naturalized as de facto law. Indeed, in the 1970s and well into the 1980s many Bosavi people assumed that any message from the mission represented the exact desires of the Papua New Guinea national government as well.

Of course the mission was also concerned with good works. It introduced a clinic at the airstrip and provided substantial health care. But with this came forms of bodily surveillance and punishment, for example refusal of aid to those who transgressed mission policies against smoking tobacco or dancing in ceremonies. A similar pattern developed with the mission school, which also introduced substantial benefit.

Nonetheless, demands that students spend long periods away from their home community undermined parental authority and disrupted family relations. Additionally, students were indoctrinated and channeled into mission-related work, and rarely rewarded or challenged in any independent areas of educational skill. Opportunities disproportionately went to those who excelled in Bible classes. The missionaries placed these students in regional Bible schools for a period of one or two years. When they returned to Bosavi, they became village pastors. With this position came considerable local power and influence, not to mention new access to resources, wealth, and deference.

The dramatic "repent or burn" message so relentlessly preached by the missionaries and their local pastors chilled somewhat by the mid- to late 1980s. This was due to government presence in Bosavi, particularly the building of a more centrally located airstrip, school, and aid post that remained outside of mission control. Missionary authority diminished as well when exploration for oil, gas, mining, and logging began to sweep through the surrounding region. With those developments Bosavi people realized that evangelical Christianity might not be the only route to social change, advantage, or opportunity.

But, in time, explorations came to reveal that there was no gold, oil, or gas to exploit on Bosavi land. For this reason, in the late 1980s and early 1990s Bosavi people became captivated by the oil project in the Lake Kutubu area to the northeast and by the clear-cut logging project south of Mt. Bosavi. Occasional infusions of cash and material wealth followed sporadic patterns of migration by young Bosavi men to work on these projects. Both the material changes and the stories that came back to Bosavi fanned the fires of local desire, and led to broader bases of conflict around real, perceived, and possible inequities. As outside companies then tried to gain access to the Bosavi forests for industrial logging, attention became fixated on debates about the meaning of development. Local politicians emerged, and some were quickly enlisted to work for the logging concerns. Non-governmental organizations also became involved. They promoted education about the environment and tried to out-maneuver the attempts by foreign operators to convince Bosavi people to sell their forest. All of a sudden local Bosavi affairs were dominated by their connection to the regional, national, and world economy. After twenty years of largely unchallenged authority, the expatriate missionaries left in 1990, declaring, "Money is god in Bosavi now."

Ultimately, lack of government presence, leadership, and local development possibilities led Bosavi people to feel increasingly alienated in the 1990s. Life took on a more anxious tone as they waited, and still wait, for something to happen. Some local Christians imagine that this something can only be an apocalyptic millennial event in the near future. Others imagine a dramatic development project, like some form of logging or mining, with extraordinary wealth matched by extraordinary physical transformation of the landscape. Others simply yearn for opportunities to participate in a cash economy, through small business and locally sustainable agriculture projects.

As desires mount and a sense of marginality escalates, Bosavi people also wonder and speculate about what hasn't happened. In that context some have developed a particular nostalgia for the practices they felt compelled to give up long ago under pressure from local pastors and the APCM missionaries. Central to this sense of loss are the abandoned ceremonies and poetic songs that were vibrant in earlier times. This is why the arena of musical loss, the Bosavi world largely represented on Disc III, is in some measure being filled in now by the local guitar band movement, the new Bosavi represented by Disc I. And throughout it all, what remains as representative as ever are the sounds and songs of everyday life and work in the forest as heard on Disc II.

RESEARCH IN BOSAVI: FURTHER READING AND LISTENING

The historical period since the mid-1960s, so turbulent with change for Bosavi, has been witnessed firsthand by three researchers.

Edward L. Schieffelin arrived in Bosavi in 1966. His first research concentrated on Bosavi ceremonialism, and in the 1970s he returned to study its demise. In the 1980s and 1990s he studied the exploration and colonial history of the region. More recently his 1990s work has documented the struggle over logging and development in the area. Some of his publications on these topics are:

The Sorrow of the Lonely and the Burning of the Dancers (St. Martin's Press, 1976).

"The End of Traditional Music, Dance, and Body Decoration in Bosavi, Papua New Guinea," in Robert Gordon, ed. *The Plight of Peripheral People in Papua New Guinea* (Cultural Survival Books, 1981).

Like People You See in a Dream (with Robert Crittenden) (Stanford University Press, 1991).

"History and the Fate of the Forest on the Great Papuan Plateau," *Anthropological Forum* 7(4): 575-597 (1997).

Bambi B. Schieffelin first went to Bosavi in 1967 and returned in the 1970s to study language acquisition and parent-child interaction. In the 1980s and 1990s she studied the development of Bosavi literacy, language change, and ideology. Some of her publications on these topics are:

"The Acquisition of Kaluli," in Dan Slobin, ed. *The Cross-Linguistic Study of Language Acquisition* (Lawrence Erlbaum, 1986).

The Give and Take of Everyday Life: Language Socialization of Kaluli Children (Cambridge University Press, 1990).

"Creating evidence: Making sense of written words in Bosavi," in Elinor Ochs et al., eds. *Grammar and Interaction* (Cambridge University Press, 1996).

"Introducing Kaluli Literacy," in Paul Kroskrity, ed. *Regimes of Language* (School of American Research Press, 2000).

Bosavi-English-Tok Pisin Dictionary (with Steven Feld, Ho:ido: Degelo:, Ho:nowo: Degili, Kulu Fuale, Ayasilo Ha:ina, and Da:ina Ha:waba:) (Australian National University, Pacific Linguistics C-153, 1998).

I joined Edward L. Schieffelin and Bambi B. Schieffelin in Bosavi in 1976–77 after listening to the sound recordings they made in 1966–68. I was moved by the power of the performances I heard and wanted to know more about the kind of creativity and imagination that animated them. My research on Bosavi song, rainforest ecology, and cultural poetics has brought me back to the region throughout the 1980s and 1990s as well. Some of my writings are:

Sound and Sentiment: Birds, Weeping, Poetics and Song in Kaluli Expression (University of Pennsylvania Press, 1982; second edition 1990).

"Aesthetics as iconicity of style, or, 'lift-up-over sounding': getting into the Kaluli groove," in Charles Keil and Steven Feld. *Music Grooves* (University of Chicago Press, 1994).

"Waterfalls of Song: An Acoustemology of Place Resounding in Bosavi, Papua New Guinea," in Steven Feld and Keith Basso, eds. *Senses of Place* (School of American Research Press, 1996).

Responding to the variety of poetic, vocal and instrumental expression I heard in Bosavi during my initial 1976–77 research, I also recorded extensively, and later edited a representative selection of local music on two LPs.

Music of the Kaluli. Institute of Papua New Guinea Studies, 1981.

The Kaluli of Papua Nugini: Weeping and Song. Barenreiter Musicaphon, 1985.

Both of these titles are now out of print; selections from them are included on Discs II and III of this collection.

Two other CDs complement this anthology. The first is a soundscape day in the life of Bosavi, featuring short segments of work, leisure, and ritual song woven into the larger sound environment of the birds, insects, waters, and other everyday rainforest ambiences. The second is an environmental sound art collection devoted exclusively to more detailed presentation of the ambiences of Bosavi birds and of everyday rainforest rhythms.

Voices of the Rainforest. Rykodisc, 1991.

Rainforest Soundwalks: Ambiences of Bosavi, Papua New Guinea. Earth Ear, 2001.

RELATED RECORDINGS ON SMITHSONIAN FOLKWAYS

The Living, Dead and Dying: Music of the New Guinea Wape, F-4269, 1978.

Music from South New Guinea, F-4216, 1971.

Stories and Poems of New Guinea Read by Bernard Barshay, Alois Jerewai, Albert Toro, Joseph Saruva, and others, F-9786, 1979.

PNG MUSIC AND THE INSTITUTE OF PAPUA NEW GUINEA STUDIES

If Papua New Guinea is renowned for its astonishing physical, cultural, and linguistic diversity — four million people and more than seven hundred and fifty different languages and cultures — it should be equally astonishing that so little of its rich musical heritage has reached beyond the region.

Location recording of New Guinea's musics date to the earliest days of sound technology, at the turn to the 20th century. Now, one hundred years later, PNG's traditional musics have only made their way into the world of global phonography on some twenty-five LPs (including two on the Smithsonian Folkways label), followed by ten CDs. By contrast a vibrant PNG popular music industry publishes a few hundred new releases each year, mostly on cassette, the main medium of local circulation. In the 1990s, music videos have also been a regular feature of the urban PNG popular music scene.

Since PNG's independence in 1975, the Music Department of the Institute of Papua New Guinea Studies has played a central role in recording, documenting, archiving, promoting, and publishing PNG music. Information on locally produced PNG cassettes plus listings for all traditional and popular PNG music recordings can be found in a 1984 IPNGS book, *Commercial Recordings of Papua New Guinea Music, 1949–1983*. Since 1984 update supplements have been issued. Among other important IPNGS publications is the eleven-cassette and book set, *Papua New Guinea Music Collection*, still the best general introduction to PNG's musical diversity. These and other IPNGS music publications can be obtained from:

IPNGS Music Department
P.O. Box 1432, Boroko, III, Papua New Guinea
phone: 675-325-4644
fax: 675-325-0531
e-mail: ipngs@global.net.pg

Institute of Papua New Guinea Studies

ACKNOWLEDGMENTS

Support for Bosavi research and recording projects in 1976–77 was provided by the Anthropology Film Center and the Archives of Traditional Music at Indiana University. Support for research and recording in the 1980s was provided by the National Science Foundation, the National Endowments for the Arts and Humanities, the Wenner-Gren Foundation for Anthropological Research, and the University of Pennsylvania. Research support in the 1990s was provided by the John D. and Catherine T. MacArthur Foundation, The University of Texas at Austin, The University of California at Santa Cruz, and New York University. I am grateful to all of these organizations and institutions, and to Bambi B. Schieffelin and Edward L. Schieffelin for many years of collaboration in and out of Bosavi.

My parents, Anita and Bob, have generously supported this work from its inception, and I dedicate this project to them. In a strange and lovely way they are quite directly responsible for my career as a sound recordist. The family recordings we made at home in the early 1950s with a not-so-portable LP disc-cutter hooked me both on sound technology and sound documentary before I was three years old.

Research affiliation throughout my years of work in Papua New Guinea has been provided by the Institute of Papua New Guinea Studies. I thank Ulli Beier for his initial invitation to work with the IPNGS, and for his tireless encouragement of PNG arts and artists. For many years of support and friendship in PNG I am particularly grateful to Don Niles of the IPNGS Music Department. My greatest PNG debt and thanks, of course, go to the people of Bosavi, especially the Bona people of Sululeb and Bolekini who have always been gracious hosts, and to my principal music teachers and guides with poetic transcription and translation: Ulahi, Yubi, Kulu, Gaso, Gigio, Hasele, Ayasilo, Da:ina, and Odo.

Author royalties from the sale of this recording go to the Bosavi People's Fund, a trust established in 1991 to support locally initiated projects and education in the Bosavi region (managed by The Tides Foundation, http://www.tides.org), and to the Music Department of the Institute of Papua New Guinea Studies, to support publication and research on PNG music.

Original recordings in 1976-77, 1982, 1984, 1990, and 1992 were made on a Nagra 4-S 1/4" tape recorder, typically with a stereo pair of AKG 451EB + CK1 or CK8 microphones. In

1994–95 and 1998–99 the original recordings were made on a Sony D7 DAT through an Aerco preamp by Jerry Chamkis, with a stereo pair of AKG 460B + CK1 microphones. Analog to digital transfer, editing, and mastering was done with Manny Rettinger at Ubik Sound, in Albuquerque, New Mexico.

CREDITS

Researched, recorded, annotated and photographed by Steven Feld

Additional Photos by Murray Rule (p. 10), Edward L. Schieffelin (p. 17) and Shari Robertson (p. 20; Disc II: CD face; Disc III: cover, inside cover lower left)

Mastered by Manny Rettinger

Sound production supervision by Pete Reiniger

Production supervised by Daniel Sheehy and D.A. Sonneborn

Production coordinated by Mary Monseur

Editorial assistance by Carla Borden

Design and layout by Sonya Cohen Cramer, Takoma Park, MD

ADDITIONAL SMITHSONIAN FOLKWAYS STAFF: Judy Barlas, manufacturing coordinator; McLean Brice, fiscal assistant; Lee Michael Demsey, fulfillment; Betty Derbyshire, financial operations manager; Erica Haskell, marketing assistant; Sharleen Kavetski, mail order manager; Helen Lindsay, customer service; Kevin Miller, fulfillment; Jeff Place, archivist; Evelyn Russell, customer service; Edme Pernia, program assistant; Ronnie Simpkins, audio specialist; John Smith, marketing specialist; Stephanie Smith, archivist.

ABOUT SMITHSONIAN FOLKWAYS

Folkways Records was founded by Moses Asch in 1948 to document music, spoken word, instruction, and sounds from around the world. In the ensuing decades, New York City-based Folkways became one of the largest independent record labels in the world, reaching a total of nearly 2,200 albums that were always kept in print.

The Smithsonian Institution acquired Folkways from the Moses Asch estate in 1987 to ensure that the sounds and the genius of the artists would be preserved for future generations. All Folkways recordings are available by special order on high-quality audio cassettes or CDs. Each recording includes the original LP liner notes.

Smithsonian Folkways Recordings was formed to continue the Folkways tradition of releasing significant recordings with high-quality documentation. It produces new titles, reissues of historic recordings from Folkways and other record labels, and in collaboration with other companies also produces instructional videotapes and recordings to accompany published books and other educational projects.

The Smithsonian Folkways, Folkways, Cook, Paredon, Monitor, Fast Folk, and Dyer-Bennet record labels are administered by the Smithsonian Institution's Center for Folklife and Cultural Heritage. They are one of the means through which the Center supports the work of traditional artists and expresses its commitment to cultural diversity, education, and increased understanding.

You can find Smithsonian Folkways Recordings at your local record store. Smithsonian Folkways, Folkways, Cook, Paredon, Fast Folk, Monitor, and Dyer-Bennet recordings are all avilable through:

Smithsonian Folkways Mail Order
750 9th Street, NW, Suite 4100,
Washington, DC 20560-0953
phone 1 (800) 410-9814 (orders only)
fax 1 (800) 853-9411 (orders only)
(Discover, MasterCard, Visa, and American Express accepted)

For further information about all the labels distributed through the Center, please consult our Internet site (www.si.edu/folkways), which includes information about recent releases, our catalogue, and a database of the approximately 35,000 tracks from more than 2,300 available recordings (click on database search). To request a printed catalogue write to the address above or e-mail folkways@aol.com